persuasive
marketing!
— Kevin Hogan

Persuading People to Buy

Insights on Marketing Psychology That Pay Off for Your Company, Professional Practice or Nonprofit Organization

Persuading People to Buy: Insights on Marketing Psychology that Pay Off for Your Company, Professional Practice or Nonprofit Organization

by Marcia Yudkin

Copyright © 2010 by Marcia Yudkin

Publisher: Creative Ways Publishing
               PO Box 305
               Goshen, MA 01032
               www.marketinginsightguides.com

Cover Design and Interior Design: Kitty Werner, RSBPress

Cover Photo: © Ilya Genkin/Fotolia.com

Author Photo: Gila Yudkin

ISBN 978-0-9716407-0-2

Printed in the United States of America

Persuading People to Buy

Insights on Marketing Psychology That
Pay Off for Your Company, Professional
Practice or Nonprofit Organization

Marcia Yudkin

Marketing Insight Guides
Creative Ways Publishing

Introduction

Years ago, I ran a class for freelance writers on how to convince top-tier magazine editors to assign them articles. One man brought in a rejection letter he'd received and read it out loud. His face turned red with anger as he reached the end.

"What a stupid, stupid editor!" the man exclaimed, slapping the letter with the hand not holding it. "I *told* him it was a national story I was proposing, not a local one. Should I send him back my letter with the sentence that said that circled?"

This person had run into a gap that exists whether you're selling ideas or iPhones, wine or weight loss coaching. It's the gap between how you think and how others do, the gap between what you believe will make others agree with you, then take a particular action and what actually persuades them (or not).

Passion alone does not bridge the gap. Often reason doesn't create interest and willingness, either.

Persuasion always begins with an understanding of the audience's expectations, beliefs, habits and desires. By far, the hardest and most necessary part of marketing is how to shift your perspective from your own thinking and perception to that of the customer. Only then can you create a connection and motivate them to buy.

The man in my class, for instance, had failed to meet the editor's criteria separating a national story from a local one. His own criteria were irrelevant.

This book contains anecdotes, explanations, tips and research findings that show how to relate your pitch, offers and pricing to what matters to those you're hoping will become—and remain—buyers.

The chapters originate in a weekly column, *The Marketing Minute*, that I've published since 1998. You can sign up for a free email subscription at www.yudkin.com/markmin.htm. I've added action steps and quotes to help you apply the marketing lessons in the columns and to enhance their impact.

Contents

Part 1

Know Your Customers

Your Audience's Expectations

Guidelines from the Boston Center for Adult Education, where I used to teach, remind teachers that even though adult learners may not have been in a classroom in decades, they come to class with specific expectations like these:

+ The classroom contains chairs with writing arms or chairs and a table.
+ The teacher knows more than students.
+ The teacher speaks from the front of the room.
+ The student takes notes on important points.

A teacher who violates these expectations has an uphill battle winning over students.

Expectations derive not only from childhood experiences, but also from the current business climate. For instance, someone now calling their insurance company on a weekend would expect to be able to leave a message, though this would not have been true 20 years ago.

Expectations also arise from your behavior with clients. If you normally call clients back within hours, they'll begin to worry whether you've had a heart attack or something if a couple of days go by without a callback.

Do you know—and meet—the expectations of the folks you attempt to sell to?

Action Steps

+ Convene a focus group and ask them to describe the way they imagine themselves experiencing your product or service. This often unearths pre-purchase expectations.

+ Survey customers a week or two after they buy, asking whether or not there were any surprises in their purchase.

+ Unsolicited complaints may reveal foiled expectations as well. Periodically sift through customer emails to discern what people didn't realize about your offerings.

Know Your Audience

When Kristen Golden moved to Amherst, Massachusetts after many fundraising successes during her 20 years in New York City, she discovered that techniques she'd mastered in the city did not work in Western Massachusetts.

+ In New York City, businesses supporting a cause want to write a check and see their names in lights, but in Western Mass., affluent donors prefer anonymity, along with hands-on involvement.

+ Donors in New York City expect flash and gloss from organizations they support. In Western Mass., donors want to see recycled paper, as little funds spent on marketing as possible and solicitations mailed to them just once a year.

+ In New York City, it might take years to get a calendar listing for an event, while in Western Mass., the local press's coverage of nonprofits is often thoughtful and in-depth.

Whether it's fundraising or marketing, understand that you're going into someone else's universe to get results. "You can't impose your preferred way of doing things on their community," Golden says. "Know the environment, understand your own vision and see where you can push beyond the prevailing mode just a little."

Action Steps

+ Remind yourself of the human tendency to assume—falsely—that what's true for you is also true for those you are marketing to.

+ Divide your customer base into one or more types of customer and for each type, list their motivators, values, preferred pace and what they most dislike.

+ Inform yourself about a geographical or professional culture from a Chamber of Commerce, consular officials, long-time residents or a professional/trade association and its publications.

A Mile in Their Shoes

The Inn at Little Washington, Virginia, which calls it-self a "culinary shrine," has a unique method of getting ready to impress the opinion shapers who make or break an establishment of its class.

Employees each choose a restaurant reviewer, then after a month's study, write a review as he or she would. "They see what we do through someone else's eyes, and in the process can't help but find flaws with our service," says owner Patrick O'Connell in *Forbes Small Business*.

To do likewise:

✦ Play the role of a customer searching for a vendor like you. Which options that come up on your first Google page attract your notice and prompt you to explore? What does that teach you?

✦ Place your book proposal sixth in a stack of seven and imagine you're a literary agent late at night or on a commuter train. In that setting, does your proposal shine or sink?

To profitably test your press release, business plan summary, trade show banner and so on, put yourself in the role of a reporter, investor or attendee.

On a Lighter Note

"Before you criticize someone, you should walk a mile in their shoes. That way when you criticize them, you are a mile away from them and you have their shoes."

— *Jack Handey*

Americans Treasure Choices

Why does the pilot on so many flights tell you "Thanks for choosing our airline"? According to Josh Hammond and James Morrison, authors of *The Stuff Americans Are Made Of*, it's because dating back to the Puritans who landed at Plymouth Rock to practice their religion freely, Americans treasure choice.

If you market to Americans, here are some ways you'll need to offer choices:

+ Features. Henry Ford's decision to provide the Model T only in black was eventually proven a mistake. Adding choices to your menu of products or services usually means adding new buyers.
+ Ways of getting in touch. Always offer as many options as you can—phone, fax, email, web site, mail, etc. That way, customers choose the option most convenient to them.

✦ Methods and terms of payment. Don't presume which choice will appeal the most. When I provide the option to spread payments over three months, there are always folks to prefer to pay the whole amount up front.

✦ Delivery format. This applies particularly to the information business, where some folks prefer to learn by reading, some by listening to audios, some through interactive seminars and others through one-on-one consulting. Price is rarely the determining factor.

Food for Thought

"It is our choices that show what we truly are, far more than our abilities."

— *J.K. Rowling*

CEO Hot Buttons

Trying to sell to CEOs? According to research by The Brooks Group, an approach that hits the hot buttons of CEOs who founded and still run their companies will backfire with CEOs hired as corporate executives. Their motivations, priorities, personal goals and decision principles differ as greatly as those of accountants and janitors.

Whereas the entrepreneurial CEOs cherish being in charge and calling the shots, the corporate CEOs treasure getting the whole team on board and spreading the risk.

Whereas the entrepreneurial CEOs prefer goods and services presented as practical and easy to implement, the corporate CEOs lean toward purchases that maintain harmony and a minimum of disruption in their company.

The entrepreneurial CEOs respond to providers who are flexible and responsive, while the corporate CEOs seek vendors with stability and respectability.

For entrepreneurial CEOs, you should justify your price by documenting its cost-effectiveness, while the corporate CEOs want pricing to be prudent and safe.

Entrepreneurial CEOs will recoil from a marketing pitch for something "standardized," while corporate CEOs will run from something presented as "revolutionary."

Know your audience! Seek out research that describes what matters to them.

Action Steps

- ✦ In your favorite search engine, look up research on your target market by typing the phrase "purchase decisions" into the search box, followed by the name of the niche.
- ✦ Visit the web sites of associations or groups to which your customers belong and look for revealing surveys, studies and editorials.
- ✦ For additional insights, chat up people who sell non-competing products and services to the same audience.

Insult One Group to Woo Another?

The headline of an advertisement in my local paper proclaimed, "Disgruntled Employees Coverage."

Two columns of type explained this new kind of coverage, officially called "employment practices liability" insurance. Clearly the insurance agency running the ad considered their name catchier, but aren't some people labeled "disgruntled employees" by employers truly wronged?

This insurance covers "defense costs, settlements and judgments related to sexual harassment, discrimination, wrongful termination and breach of contract," said the ad. It came close to saying that anyone bringing such a case was trying to "get even."

Chills ran down my spine. The ad ran in a general newspaper, read by thousands of employees and their family members who buy homeowners and car insurance from someone in the area. Even someone in the employer group might feel offended by this attitude.

What undoubtedly sounded clever and candid when the person writing the ad was thinking of a certain audience ran the risk of repelling many other readers who undoubtedly were also either actual or potential customers.

Remember who will actually receive your marketing message, so you don't shoot yourself in the foot.

Action Steps

+ Before approving any ad, brochure, blog post or news release, ask yourself whether anything bad might happen if someone other than the intended audience read it. If so, reconsider your message.

+ When you have two diametrically opposed audiences, such as employers and employers or students and teachers, reach out to the populations separately via in-group magazines or group-specific mailings.

Purple Cows and Brown Ones

As someone celebrating my one-year anniversary of moving to the country, I was startled to read this sentiment in Seth Godin's book, *Purple Cow: Transform Your Business By Being Remarkable:*

"Cows, after you've seen them for a while, are boring, They may be perfect cows, attractive cows, cows with great personalities, cows lit by beautiful light, but they're still boring."

What startled me was not the opinion—many city dwellers find woods and farmland boring—but the opinion stated as a fact. Godin goes on to base his entire book on the premise that if you don't capture attention by standing out from the crowd (as a purple cow does), you're doomed.

It's false and dangerous to assume that if you constantly crave something new, everyone else who matters does too.

It's equally shaky to assume that people who flock to what's new and different are the most profitable customers to have. Maybe yes, maybe no. Those who prefer what's familiar (like brown cows) might be more loyal and require less customer service than so-called early adopters.

Study your marketplace. Don't assume!

Food for Thought

"All the good ideas I ever had came to me while I was milking a cow."

— *American painter Grant Wood*

Gender Differences in Shopping

It's become almost a cliché to talk about men hating to ask for directions when they drive. But according to Paco Underhill, author of *Why We Buy: The Science of Shopping*, men equally rarely ask for the department they want in a store. They'd rather wander around lost and leave if they can't find it. Undoubtedly men behave the same way reading a marketing brochure or visiting a web site.

Underhill notes some other gender differences in retail shopping:

- ✦ Of shoppers who tried something on, 65 percent of the men bought it, versus 25 percent of the women.
- ✦ While 86 percent of women shoppers looked at price tags, only 72 percent of men did.
- ✦ At the supermarket, almost all women have brought a shopping list, but only 25 percent of the men did.

✦ Women particularly hate being jostled from behind and may leave a store without buying if aisles are too narrow.

Whether we sell in a retail, one-on-one or virtual environment, we tend to assume everyone resembles us. It ain't necessarily so! Stay alert and observe, instead of assuming.

On a Lighter Note

"Men are from Mars. Women are from Venus. Computers are from hell."

— *Anonymous*

Surprising Gender Senders

"My clients are 95 percent men," another marketing consultant told me. "I have a very aggressive style—maybe that explains why."

It could be the teaching stories and emotional tone of my colleague's pitches that his male clients are responding to. More subtle cues could be contributing to this result, as well.

According to research by University of Texas psychologist James W. Pennebaker, gender differences in style come out not only in what we say but also in the kinds of words we use.

Statistically, women use more pronouns, verbs, social words, negations and references to psychological processes than men do. Men tend to use more articles, prepositions, numbers and big words than women do.

These patterns hold in hundreds of thousands of essays, blogs and conversations tallied by Pennebaker's computers.

Additionally, people's choice of pronouns tends to change dramatically when they are under stress.

For marketers, these findings are tantalizing. Pennebaker notes it's hard to consciously control those little "function words" in conversation and spontaneous writing. So far this research tells us what words reveal, but not how they influence.

Action Steps

+ Show your marketing copy to a group of people who don't know you or your business. Ask them whether they think it was written by a man or a woman. Consider then whether or not that's the answer that's appropriate for that product or service.

+ Ask also whether they think your marketing copy is directed toward men or women, and what clues in the text lead them to think so.

Do You Really Know Your Customers?

Are you certain you know who's buying your stuff? Mandy MacMullan, owner of a custom jewelry business called Tigerlilly Design, made an eye-opening discovery when she began surveying shoppers at her CustomTiaras.com site to ask what kind of occasion they were looking for a tiara for.

"I thought the majority of visitors to my site were brides," she says. "But about half of those who've turned in questionnaires were teenagers looking for tiaras for their proms. I'd been catering to brides in the designs, but now I'm going to add a new line for proms—funkier, more colorful, a bit less expensive and hipper.

"Basically, this is a big opportunity for me to expand. So far, 99 percent of my sales have been to brides, but not because they're the only ones coming to my site (as I originally thought). Rather, they're the only group I'm catering to right now."

Might you be overlooking a market that is already coming to you but leaving unsatisfied? Chatting up shoppers, if you see them in person, or adding an online survey to your web site could reveal a surprising opportunity.

Try developing your own cast of prospect characters!

Action Steps

+ If you have a well-trafficked web site, check out its demographics at Alexa.com. This service ranks the several hundred thousand most popular sites online and summarizes the gender, age, marital status, education and location of their visitors.

+ If Alexa.com doesn't track your site, look up the demographics of a popular competitor. You might discover facts that point to opportunities, such as a large number of site visitors from Ireland or an overwhelming percentage of people with children.

+ Use an online survey company to post a brief questionnaire about why people came to your site, what they were hoping to find and what they would use your wares to do.

Never Sell to Androids

A *Marketing Minute* subscriber asked: "How do I borrow great ideas for selling products to consumers and apply them when selling to businesses?"

It's important to recognize some differences in selling to people buying for personal use and those buying for their company. In the company situation:

+ The purchaser may be buying for staff members, not himself or herself. You need careful writing that doesn't assume the "you" who is buying is the one who will be taking the seminar, using the software or reading and applying the report.

+ More people may be involved in a purchase decision. You must anticipate what the person who must approve the purchase wants to know, as well as questions of the one who originally found your information.

✦ The stakes may be higher. In the company context, jobs and million-dollar projects may be on the line.

✦ Licensing opportunities may apply. Head off someone sharing your information product with the whole company by stating fees for multiple users.

Nevertheless, it's humans, not "a company" that decides to buy. Write accordingly.

Action Steps

✦ Even if you gather leads and sell online, there's no substitute for getting up close and personal with your buyers. Find someone local who's a potential customer, invite them to lunch and have them describe in detail what prompts them every step of the way from looking for a solution to the problem you solve to buying.

✦ With your informant, show them small sections of your marketing pitches and ask, "Is this relevant to you?" "Is it on target?" If not, "What should we have talked about instead here?"

Wooing One Important Customer

Do you need to gain the attention of and win over one very important person? Author Ray Simon calls this "business courtship" and offers creative ways to approach a potential business partner, investor, employer or client who is normally hard to reach or persuade.

Cosmetics mogul Estee Lauder began supplying Galleries Lafayette in Paris after spilling her fragrance Youth Dew on the floor of the store so that the resistant manager could witness the crowd's interest.

Broadway casting director Michael Shurtleff got his first break by writing a chatty letter to producer David Merrick week after week. Despite never receiving a reply, he increased his missives to twice a week. After seven months, Merrick invited him to come in and gave him a job.

Random House founder Bennett Cerf pasted reviews praising it as great literature within the copy of James Joyce's purportedly obscene book *Ulysses* that would be seized by Customs officials. Those snuck-in reviews helped persuade the judge to allow the book into the U.S.

Read about these examples and scores more in Ray Simon's entertaining book, *Mischief Marketing.*

❧   ❧

Food for Thought

"Fortune favors the bold."

— Virgil (70–19 BC)

High-Value Marketing

Some marketers worship at the shrine of "response rate" or "conversion rate." Where high-value clients and partnership opportunities are concerned, this is a big mistake.

When each client is worth $5,000 or more, you should unleash your imagination in getting their attention and put persistence into overdrive. Some ideas:

+ Create and send a laminated, personalized newspaper article lauding the achievements the client would achieve after using your products or services.
+ Send promotional items personalized with their name and tied thematically to the benefit you offer, then follow up with a call.
+ Research the personal or business interests of a target and send relevant articles week after week with a personal note.

Product development specialist Bob Serling recalls the time he eyed a prospect that trained more than 800,000 people a year. "It took 31 contacts to get them to take our demo," he says. "If I had quit after eight attempts, we would have lost a high-value customer. My guideline is to forget about averages and keep at it until the prospect either becomes a customer or says they aren't interested."

Action Steps

+ Interview several long-term, lucrative clients on what they remember about the process of deciding to do business with you. How long did it take from a first contact to a first deal?

+ Increase the frequency, number and types of contacts with your prospects. If you normally call to follow up, try email and mail as well. If you normally just email, add phone, mail and fax communications—always friendly and low-pressure in tone.

What People Say Vs. What They Do

At adult education centers nationwide, many students say they want follow-up courses, but such courses consistently get low enrollment.

For many years, marketers' surveys showed that a majority preferred HTML format over plain text. But when offered a choice, those receiving plain-text newsletters wouldn't switch.

As anyone who's either been a parent or had one knows, there's an enormous difference between what we say and what we do. That's why actual testing—giving people a chance to buy or observing how consumers behave in certain circumstances—is always more reliable than gathering opinions. Don't bet the farm based on opinion polls, focus groups or questionnaire feedback alone.

John Forde, a New York City copywriter, recalls asking a room full of customers which direct-mail promo packages on the table they found appealing. Everyone prefaced their remarks with "Well, I never respond to junk mail, but..."

"That was interesting," says Forde, "since every one of them had been invited because they were our best direct-mail buyers. Buyers are not fully aware of their own consumer behavior."

∽ ∾

On a Lighter Note

"In theory, there is no difference between theory and practice. But in practice, there is."

— *Yogi Berra*

Picture Your Customer

When asked whom he writes for, novelist John Updike once replied, "For a precocious twelve-year-old in Kansas." He painted a vivid word picture of this kid, whom he'd obviously envisioned in detail.

Some successful businesses do the same by developing a precise profile of an archetypal customer, complete with name, age, occupation, passions, dislikes and idiosyncrasies. Pioneering software developer Alan Cooper describes this so-called persona process in his book, *The Inmates are Running the Asylum*, which explains how to make software suit how people think and act rather than vice versa.

"We don't say that Emilee uses business software," he says. "Emilee uses WordPerfect Version 5.1 to write letters to Gramma. We don't let Emilee drive to work. We give her a dark-blue 1991 Toyota Camry, with a gray plastic kid's seat strapped into the back and an ugly scrape on the rear bumper."

With such specifics, these fictional individuals come alive for the software designers, who then artfully anticipate users' desires rather than present solutions not needed by the target market.

Action Steps

+ Go through a pile of magazines and cut out photos that personify your customers. Give each one a name and tack them on the wall behind your computer. Daydream about their daily lives; spin stories about them.

+ With your colleagues, role-play conversations between your personified customers and people they encounter before, during and after using your product or service. Have fun with it, while trying to stay in character.

Use Customers' Words

Marketing succeeds almost effortlessly when you use the words, categories and reasoning instinctively used by your most likely buyers.

Career counselor Joan Cousins of Pittsfield, Massachusetts, didn't leave this to chance. For two years, she kept track of the terminology employed by those who hired her services. When they called, they did not say, "I need career counseling." Instead, 80 to 90 percent used one of two other very specific phrases.

Cousins then composed an ad highlighting one of those key phrases. "That ad brings me an average of one very serious inquiry a week, which about 80 percent of the time turns into a multi-session client," she says.

To gather powerful word use data like Cousins', you can:

✦ Listen to new clients, as Cousins did.

- ✦ Ask previous clients what prompted them to take action to buy when they did.
- ✦ When you meet people who patronize a competing service provider, ask them what need prompted them to hire them.
- ✦ If you have a new-client questionnaire, ask people what they're hoping to get from your business relationship.

On a Lighter Note

"I once used the word *obsolete* in a headline, only to discover that 43 per cent of housewives had no idea what it meant. In another headline, I used the word *ineffable,* only to discover that I didn't know what it meant myself."

— *David Ogilvy*

Part 2
Establishing Value

Reputation Pays

According to RainToday.com's *Fees and Pricing Benchmark Report: Consulting Industry 2008*, based on surveying 645 consulting firms, standing taller among one's peers carries distinct rewards:

"Firms that are well known in their target markets receive higher fees, see their revenue grow, and are more likely to be profitable than firms that are not as well known in their target markets."

If you wish to reap those rewards, you have three routes to top-of-mind status. Each route has a different answer to the question, "Who says you're great?"

1. Word of mouth, where scuttlebutt within the industry says you're great.
2. Publicity, where the media anoint you as a leader.
3. Marketing, where you anoint yourself as worthy.

Each route has different costs and dynamics. Word of mouth works slowly, demands disciplined quality and tends to last—unless turnover in the field is high. Publicity requires cleverness and initiative; when repeated, it also has a lasting effect. Marketing requires the highest investment, has the least credibility, and stops working when the spending stops.

Which route are you on? If none, you're working harder than you need to.

Food for Thought

"It's when you play safe that you create a world of utmost insecurity."

— *Dag Hammarskjold*

They Don't Value What I Do!

What if there are zillions of companies out there that need your skills but don't realize they need your skills? This question came up recently with a woman who has 14 years of technical editing experience but was in despair. From her point of view, so many companies urgently need someone to clean up and clarify their prose, but they won't act on this need. They don't get the value of effective written communication.

Likewise, suppose you're a magician with house plants. But office managers keep telling you, "Geez, so what if our plants are diseased and dying?"

Forget about trying to persuade people to value what you value. You can break through this kind of resistance only by demonstrating that what you're good at helps them accomplish some objective that they do hold dear. Tell the companies that spew out atrocious grammar that you'll win them greater credibility with investors. If you're the green thumb, tell managers that you improve productivity by creating a healthy, reassuring indoor environment.

Pitch yourself to companies in terms of what they know they want, and you boost the chances that they'll want you.

Action Steps

+ List all the benefits (outcomes, advantages) your company offers. Create another list of what your target market would like to achieve. Find one or more commonalities on the two lists and use those for your marketing pitch.

+ If you find nothing in common, look closer for items on each list that you can relate to one another in some way, and see if you can make that connection convincing.

+ If you strike out on finding commonalities on the lists, find another target market!

Sell to Those Who Grasp Your Value

Last week I finished reading the novel *Peace Like a River*, by Lief Enger. Its luminous portrayal of appealing characters had me marveling at the author's skill and sensitivity at least every other page. I rushed to tell my friends who love books to read it.

Note that I did not urge friends who do not adore books to read it.

This simple example points toward a way to make every marketing dollar well spent when the economy turns tough: Market primarily to people who already understand the value of what you sell.

- Contact past customers, who are five times more likely to respond than non-customers.
- Contact knowledgeable or specialized prospects, for instance by advertising in magazines for experts or enthusiasts.

✦ Contact new people through speaking engagements sponsored by sophisticated special-interest organizations.

✦ Contact influential colleagues and media people who know you and might take it upon themselves to educate prospective buyers.

✦ Contact current clients and ask if they know others who would benefit from your products or services.

✦ Contact prospective customers who don't know you but match the profile of your best clients.

Food for Thought

"When you see a swordsman, draw your sword. Do not recite poetry to one who is not a poet."

— *Zen proverb*

Your Value, Understood, Part I

A *Marketing Minute* subscriber asks: "Invariably once we finish a project, our customers say the work was worth many times what they paid. But getting them to understand the value ahead of time is hard. Any suggestions?"

Steve Slaunwhite has a great suggestion in his co-authored book, *The Wealthy Freelancer*. Ask the "expected results question," he advises. "The more you position your services around the results you can help a client achieve, the more likely you are to get the job—at the price you want."

Slaunwhite's examples of how to ask include:

+ What exactly do you need this press release to accomplish?
+ What do you need this email newsletter to accomplish for your company?

Be sure you restate their answer within your project proposal, he notes. It greatly increases the odds of a "yes."

I love this idea because it uses the client's own thinking to persuade them that an investment is worthwhile. (In a way, it helps them convince themselves.)

Signed testimonials from customers who explain the value of their purchase in ways others can relate to also help with this challenge.

Food for Thought

"The aim of marketing is to know and understand the customer so well, the product or service fits him and sells itself."

— Peter Drucker

Your Value, Understood, Part II

Pitches for expensive products often include indicators of what a component or bonus would cost if we bought it separately, such as "(Value: $738)."

When people can actually purchase the component or bonus separately, the value is a straightforward fact. However, in many cases a monetary estimate of something's value is concocted out of thin air—and customers realize that.

Here's another approach.

As reported in the book *Yes! 50 Scientifically Proven Ways to Be Persuasive,* a home improvement company increased sales of its $15,000 backyard hot tubs by more than 500 percent by saying (truthfully) that many buyers reported the spa was like having an extra room in their house. They then invited people to consider how much it would cost to expand their house with another room.

Interested customers perform a just-for-them mental calculation and convince themselves.

More examples of this process:

+ "Typically, our software enables one staff member to do the work of three."
+ "Of people who move to Homeville, 79 percent give up their car and say they don't miss it."

Action Steps

+ Look through your customer feedback for non-monetary indicators of the value they experienced from your work.
+ Create a survey for recent clients asking them what they were able to do or have as a result of what they purchased from you.
+ In sales presentations and marketing copy, invite potential buyers to imagine what it's worth to them to have 20 percent more patient appointments, increased name recognition or whatever outcomes were mentioned in the testimonials and survey.

When They Don't Get It

Usually this complaint comes from the proud produc-
ers of a cool new whoozywhatsit: "Our system has so
many incredible bells and whistles, but customers won't buy."
Or "When they see what our product does, they say 'Nice!'
but not 'I want one.'"

The remedy requires working backward from what the
new thing does to why someone should want it. What problem does it solve?

Begin your marketing pitch with the problem. Dramatize
that dilemma with scenarios from your prospective customers' nightmares or day-to-day realities. Show how your product solves this problem. Tell them how to buy or take the
next step toward a purchase.

Sometimes my clients believe they're following this for-
mula, but they're still focused on their thing's features. The
problem you want to play up is not "I want anti-lock brakes"

or "I want less stopping distance" but "I want to drive safely on icy roads and be able to avoid an accident if a dog or a kid jumps in front of my car."

Instead of starting with "what," tackle "why" to prompt "I want one!"

᠀ ᠀

Action Steps

+ Convene a group of friends or family members and explain to them what your product or service does. Then ask them who would want it, and why. Sometimes they can instinctively put into words what has eluded you.

+ Also ask your feedback group what the item reminds them of. Sometimes this brings up a metaphor that helps customers-to-be nod and reach for their wallets.

Part 3
Reasons for Buying

Using Hot Button Appeals

With marketing experience, you inevitably experience some promotions succeeding beyond your expectations while others klunk without much response at all.

How to understand the difference? A new book, *Hot Button Marketing* by Barry Feig, provides a useful framework for guessing possible reasons for such variations in response. Then you can tweak intelligently and try again.

Feig profiles 16 emotional drives that motivate people today to buy, including familiar ones like the desire to belong and the urge to be superior to others, along with newer wants like re-evaluating priorities and reinventing oneself.

In examining the web copy that quickly filled my first "Launch Your Information Empire" action group, I see that I repeatedly referred to a dream becoming reality, which corresponds to Feig's hot button #16, wish fulfillment.

Those who signed up resonated with that theme. Note that I did not muck up the presentation with appeals to status seeking (Feig's hot button #2) or instant gratification (#12). Tossing disparate hot buttons together doesn't work.

Action Steps

+ To warm up to the idea of emotional hot buttons, go to your closet at home and pull out four items of clothing you haven't worn in a year. Then ask yourself: Why did I buy this? Why have I kept it? Listen for wishes, hopes and fears in your answers.

+ Get a bunch of friends together and open up the Yellow Pages to a random page. Imagine that you had to compete with those vendors with an offering that cost twice as much as theirs. How would you persuade customers to prefer doing business with you? Repeat on another page. What did you learn about emotional reasons for buying?

Multiple Hot Buttons

After reading last week's *Marketing Minute* on hot buttons, several subscribers asked: "You said not to jumble together disparate hot buttons, but what if customers have markedly different reasons for buying?"

When some buy an exercise machine to feel better about themselves, while others wish to reach their fitness goals and still others want to avoid fighting crowds to and at the gym, use sequential marketing.

Through a series of direct mail pieces or multiple ads within a short period of time to the same audience, focus each message on just one hot button. Today they receive the "feel younger" pitch, next week the "get fit faster" pitch and the week after, the "no more traffic jams" pitch.

At a web site, which people may visit just once, headline it with the strongest or most common hot button. Feature the other hot buttons in quotes, case studies and lists, set off from the main presentation.

To identify the strongest hot buttons, test headlines against each other or ask buyers what got them to take the leap. Often themes emerge in their replies.

Action Steps

+ Create a free report related to what you sell. Sign up for a Google Adwords account, if you don't already have one. Create at least three little text ads for your report that appeal to different emotional needs. Test these against each other to find out which hot button reigns supreme in your market.

+ Once you've identified your strongest text ad, create another version of it for the same report that's somewhat more rational and straight-laced, and yet another version with more emotional hot sauce. Then test these against each other to determine what level of enthusiasm clicks most with your crowd.

Emotional Reasons for Buying

If you'd like to charge premium prices and trigger longing for your product or service, fuel the dreams of customers, advises Gian Luigi Longinotti-Buitoni, CEO of Ferrari North America and author of a fascinating book, *Selling Dreams*.

While speed-demon Ferraris are clearly luxuries, dreams don't have to cost a fortune, says Longinotti-Buitoni, citing Volkswagen's revived Beetle, which flew out of showrooms by enabling Baby Boomers to relive the 1960s.

If you think your product or service is too functional to ignite dreams, consider how people can buy a thing or choose their vendor for emotional reasons.

Book: In 1989 many bought Salman Rushdie's *The Satanic Verses* not to read it but to strike a blow for civilization in the face of the death threats against him.

Vacation: Pay top dollar to get cold, dirty, exhausted and in danger? Some do to satisfy their dream of adventure.

Legal services: People might hire the attorney who speaks to their dream of revenge.

Cell phone: To some, not for talking but to feel safe.

What does your customer long for?

On a Lighter Note

"I still believe that one can learn to play the piano by mail and that mud will give you a perfect complexion."

— *Zelda Fitzgerald*

Cherchez le Sentiment

Remember those whodunits where the detective exclaims "Cherchez la femme!" (Look for the woman) and the mystery finally untwists to a satisfying conclusion?

According to Linda Goodman and Michelle Helin, authors of *Why Customers Really Buy: Uncovering the Emotional Triggers That Drive Sales,* we should pay less attention to what customers say than to their behavior while saying it.

Pay little attention to commentary delivered in a deliberate, factual, neutral manner, they say. Pursue responses that are longer, livelier and more personal, delivered with direct eye contact, voice inflections and animated gestures.

The latter represent clues to the values, needs, beliefs, feelings and experiences that truly drive buying behavior.

Goodman and Helin recommend open-ended questions asked face to face to uncover the unexpected motivations that lead people to care or not care and act this way or that.

In their case studies, they show how feelings like fear, resentment, embarrassment, betrayal, anger, worry and indifference can sabotage marketing and fundraising efforts.

By using insights into emotional triggers, companies can shift their positioning, remove hidden obstacles, tweak offers and better connect with customers.

ॐ ॐ

Action Steps

+ At a networking meeting or any other business get-together, identify the difference between people discussing something they very much care about and those delivering their information from habit. How did you tell which was which?

+ When talking face to face with a client, stay alert for the behaviors that signal caring and commitment. Then feed that spark so it grows to a glow. Pay close attention to what the client is saying when he or she is most animated. Tuck away that part of the conversation for reflection afterwards.

Today's Upscale Motivators

P eople buy on emotion and justify their purchase with logic." A new book contributes depth and currency to this long-accepted truth about marketing and sales. *Trading Up: The New American Luxury,* by Michael Silverstein and Neil Fiske, discusses particular emotions now motivating people to buy high-priced products:

✦ Taking Care of Me. Overstressed people may feel they deserve products and services that pamper them and that help them feel refreshed and rejuvenated.

✦ Connecting with Friends, Mates and Family. In today's increasingly anonymous world, people will spend serious amounts of money to attract, maintain and nurture family and friends or a romantic partner.

✦ Questing. Consumers today appreciate adventure, learning, mastery and fun and are willing to pay top dollar to dream about and experience those qualities.

✦ Individual Style. High-priced products often help buyers express their personal taste, differentiate themselves from others and demonstrate their sophistication.

If you can appeal to these motivators in your sales copy and marketing strategies and back that up with genuine substance, you'll earn zealous customer loyalty and a larger share of buyers' discretionary income.

❧　❧

Food for Thought

"Some people think luxury is the opposite of poverty. It is not. It is the opposite of vulgarity."

— *Coco Chanel*

Customer Convenience as a Lure

Customer convenience rules! Consider these outstanding examples from *1,001 Ways to Keep Customers Coming Back* by Donna Greiner and Theodore B. Kinni. By making things easier for buyers, these techniques encourage repeat business, sales to a new population and customer loyalty.

+ Cracker Barrel Old Country Stores encourages highway travelers to choose this chain again on their trip by renting audio books that are returnable for credit or exchange at any other Cracker Barrel Old Country Store.

+ For theater lovers who don't like to get dressed up, brave the weather and worry about parking, a company called Globalstage offers a subscription series of plays-on-video, delivered one every couple of months.

✦ Chase Manhattan enables credit-card customers to decide when they want to receive their bill—the beginning, middle or end of the month.

✦ Chase also offers the option of the Lens Card, a credit card with a magnifier built in. It eliminates the need to lug around reading glasses to read the bil. And with the card in hand, how do you think those customers pay the bill?

Action Steps

✦ Ask least three of your best clients for ten minutes of their time, then ask them what you can do to make your products or services easier or more convenient for them.

✦ Find an online forum or discussion list where people like your customers congregate, and ask them who among the companies they do business with is most convenient to do business with and why. Often great ideas come from industries quite different from yours.

Four Ways to Discover Hot Buttons

What's the biggest worry currently for people in a certain industry? Tune into this, and you have a powerful theme for an article, press release, special offer or your web site copy. When that industry is one you target but do not directly participate in, try these methods of discovering its hot buttons:

- ✦ Attend an industry meeting or conference and during the coffee breaks, ask everyone what their biggest challenge or obstacle is this year.
- ✦ Find a discussion list or discussion board for the industry and note both heated debates and thoughtful questions experienced folks ask each other.
- ✦ Take previous clients in that industry out to lunch and ask them about current controversies in their field and any others they think are bound to break out soon.

✦ Sometimes a hot button is perennial rather than new. Simply ask your informants what business issue has most kept them awake at night over the years.

With all this listening, pay attention to the words people use to describe their fears and ordeals and echo them when you create your new product or promotion.

Action Steps

✦ Use your findings from the process described above to pitch yesterday's products with today's hot buttons.

✦ Whenever you discover a new hot button that doesn't seem to have gotten much public attention yet, write a white paper or create a video about it and distribute a press release about the white paper or video to your industry and the general news media.

Discover Distinctive Reasons to Buy

In preparation for my latest web site makeover, I toured about a dozen competitors' web sites, in search of ideas I could use or definitely wouldn't want to use at my new site. Since I'm not a potential client for them, I normally didn't spend much time looking at marketing consultants' or copywriters' web sites.

To my surprise, I discovered two sites containing a statement along these lines: "Confidential projects require a 100% surcharge." Without the surcharge, clients could see the work they'd commissioned and paid for dissected, discussed and shown off in the consultant's courses and portfolio.

Never in a million years would it have occurred to me to present confidentiality as a competitive advantage, as something all my clients receive without any extra charge.

Reading competitors' terms and conditions might be similarly eye-opening for you. Industry norms that you take for granted pertaining to privacy, quality control or courtesies for clients might have slipped while you've been quietly doing business traditionally.

"Unlike other companies, we...": See if you can create a powerful differentiator.

Action Steps

✦ Often outsiders have an easier time perceiving interesting elements you take for granted. Examine your testimonials and any media coverage you've received for observations that seemed to be stating the obvious.

✦ Invite the most curious or inquisitive person you know and give them a tour of your facility. Take note of any questions or comments they make that surprise you.

✦ Ask clients who previously did business with one or more competitors how you are different from the others.

Not Obvious, Not Shared

Yesterday a software entrepreneur called to ask if I'd play guinea pig for his new content development software. I replied, "Look, from what you said I'm skeptical, but I'll give you five minutes."

Passionately the guy launched into an explanation of what his creation could accomplish, and repeatedly I stopped him. "Whoa! Back up. How would that benefit me?"

After almost half an hour, I understood that the real aim of his software was completely different from what he'd first said. I'd pointed out half a dozen missing steps in his logic, where I remained unconvinced that his software would save me time and bring me results in a manner consistent with my values.

He in turn was incredulous when he said, "You're a writer, don't you want to make as much as possible from your writing?" and I replied, "No. If something would damage my hard-earned reputation for good writing, I'm not interested."

Create a product, and you've done only part of the work necessary to bring it to market. Assume that everyone knows what you do and thinks like you, and success will elude you.

Food for Thought

"It may take forever to win people over by persuasion, but that's quicker than you can do it by force."

— Anonymous

Creating More Reasons to Buy

It's easier to persuade people who've bought from you before to buy more than to acquire a totally new customer. If you've heard this already, consider a new wrinkle on the principle offered in a terrific book by Sergio Zyman, *The End of Marketing As We Know It.*

"If you want them to keep coming back for more and with increasing frequency, give them more and more reasons to buy beyond the apparent or the original selling proposition," he says.

For example, people usually drank Coke to slake their thirst and feel refreshed. Then Zyman and his cohorts created ads around a list of 35 reasons people might want a Coke. Sales jumped 50 percent in the next five years.

Let's suppose you're selling a book. The obvious reason to buy would be to read it. But people could also buy it to give as a gift, to own a to-be-valuable first edition, to lend copies to clients, to donate to libraries or battered women's shelters, to show it off at seminars, to present a copy to their doctor, and...?

Action Steps

+ Run a contest, asking customers to submit videos, photos or blog posts documenting how they use your product or service, with prizes for the most unusual or humorous examples.

+ For inspiration, Google "101 Reasons to Buy an Island." Then brainstorm your own list.

Rethink Your Rationale?

According to *USA Today*, the US Mint is spending $12 million to test whether Americans will finally warm up to a dollar coin, which they have rejected for decades, by pitching it as environmentally friendlier than the paper bill. (Greener than the so-called "greenback"? Slang is against them.)

Coca-Cola, which for ages touted its taste, has a new tag line: "No artificial flavors, no added preservatives. Since 1886." (Clever and informative, since most of us consider soft drinks unhealthy.)

Collections of KenKen puzzles, a new variant of Sudoku, carry the claim that they make you smarter, building on popularized studies showing that mental challenges keep the brain in shape. (Just plain fun isn't enough, I guess.)

If you're pitching your products and services the same way you did four years ago, maybe it's time to try a different rationale. Here are a few additional ideas with current appeal:

✦ Reduces your carbon footprint
✦ Helps the local economy
✦ Increases the likelihood of keeping your job
✦ Having to do more with less?

Consider adding fresh, up-to-the-season reasons to buy.

Action Steps

✦ Find or buy a small notebook. Then tomorrow, throughout the day, pay attention to all the ads that come your way. Jot down the reasons to buy presented in each ad. The day after tomorrow, scan through your list for at least three fresh reasons to buy that might make sense for your business.

✦ Go to Trendhunter.com and browse its lists and sublists of trend reports. Phrases like "experiential eating," "hobbitats," "nerdy nuptials" and "pity journaling" will jolt your creative thinking into overdrive.

Analyze Purchasing Triggers

An ad in my local paper last week showed a silver-haired couple with small children, headlined: "This Christmas, understand what your grandkids are saying!" The ad copy reminded the reader that last holiday season, they didn't relate well to their grandchildren because they couldn't hear them clearly. This year, with a [brand name] hearing aid, they'll re-establish those all-important bonds.

The technique here is simple but powerful: Analyze the situations that prompt your customers to do something about a need that might have existed for quite a while. Then refer to those triggers, explicitly or subtly, singly or multiply, in your marketing copy.

Discovering your customers' triggers can be as simple as chatting them up or as formal as a "check all that apply" survey. The crucial question: What happened to make you want to take action now?

An image consultant might find that upcoming job promotions, impending divorces, milestone birthdays and college reunions prompt clients to update their wardrobe. For a computer security firm, triggers might be news reports of hack attacks or compilation of annual reports.

Food for Thought

"To every thing there is a season, and a time to every purpose."

— Ecclesiastes

Part 4
Persuasive Techniques

Selling Through Consequences

Like many marketing experts, I recommend you tell prospective customers or clients not just what they can buy but what they get by buying. In the lingo, they purchase not because of your product or service's features but because of the benefits.

Sales trainer Dan Seidman, author of *The Death of 20th Century Selling*, suggests a twist on this. Rather than benefits, he advocates telling prospects about consequences—bad things that could or will happen until they buy what you're selling. For instance, for someone thinking of buying a car, the following would be consequences of not doing so:

+ Can't take a client to lunch in your car
+ A look that says you're not successful
+ Danger when merging in traffic
+ Feeling every bump in the road
+ Surprised by what breaks down every month

Seidman notes that for business buyers, consequences include both repercussions for the company (angry shareholders) and for the individual responsible for the purchase (lower personal income).

Try painting a vivid picture that propels folks to avoid such effects. For you, the consequence is then something to smile about.

Action Steps

+ Sit down with a paper and pad and list every consequence of not buying a particular item of yours that you can think of: dangers, hassles, costs of delay, lost opportunities and any other negative experiences.

+ Select one of those consequences and build an email, postcard or print ad campaign around it.

Make the Consequences Explicit

Losing gobs of money, the hospital one mile from where I live is slated to close. I've seen this in headlines for more than a month, but the news didn't hit home. Boston has a zillion hospitals, and this one isn't world-class.

Then I learned what the hospital closing will do to emergency service for people calling 911 in my town: The nearest other hospitals, now overburdened, could refuse heart attack or accident victims and send them a half-hour farther away. Yikes! Now I understood. Conceivably, a family member or neighbor of mine might die because of this hospital closing.

While that consequence is logical to me, I didn't draw that conclusion on my own. A similar stoppage occurs in marketing: We fail to point out consequences explicitly, thinking the implications of what we offer are obvious.

For instance, don't assume people know what can happen if off-the-shelf software misses deductions or leaves out crucial explanations it's better to provide. Spell out the consequences of not hiring your tax preparation service, and more clients may bite.

Tell them—make it plain!

❧ ☙

Action Steps

+ Slowly read through the printout of a promotional piece you've been using and highlight or circle every reason you've cited for your prospect to buy. Then for each reason, ask what the implications of that reason are for the buyer. Good prompts to use are "so that..." and "which means that..."

+ Ask your sales people and customer service representatives which consequences they think motivate people most and which rarely come up but might have an impact if they did. Then tweak your marketing pitches accordingly.

+ Turn your list of consequences into a quiz that you post on your web site or incorporate into an ad or mailing. Headline it: "Which of these concern you?"

Convince Us!

Last week I asked for social media success stories on a number of lists and received some blustery yet unpersuasive replies along these lines:

"We've had some great successes using MySpace."

Compare that to these snippets from *Marketing Minute* subscribers:

"When I started adding video, someone who had been a client for nearly seven years called me crying, she was so moved by my passion and sincerity. Then she gave me her credit card number to purchase more services." — Donna Maria Coles Johnson

"At least half of my income is generated from clients I met or befriended on social networking sites." — Nancy Marmelejo

"My five mindful eating videos to date have generated a larger audience, bigger mailing list, way more Google listings, increased CD sales, and a client waiting list. A *Boston Globe* article about my Twinkie video was syndicated nationwide and appeared in so many periodicals I've lost count." — Jean Fain

Instead of vague bragging, these communications offered specific details, a dramatic story, numbers.

These elements convince, whether you want to win over media gatekeepers or potential customers.

Food for Thought

"One woman will brag about her children, while another complains about hers; they could probably swap children without swapping tunes."

— Unknown

Surprise, Surprise

To gain attention and earn credibility, defy common sense.

Participants in my recently completed copywriting course understood why unlikely sounding claims get attention, but pressed me to explain why these would make a presentation more believable.

When we hear a surprising claim from someone who appears to know what he or she is talking about, we want to know more, figuring the expert wouldn't play reckless games with their reputation. A surprising claim like these:

- From a financial planner: To finance your retirement, don't buy stocks, bonds or mutual funds.
- From a physician: To live longer, sleep less than six hours a night.
- From an environmentalist: Recycling does more harm than good.

(I've invented these to illustrate the point. Maybe they're true, maybe they're false.)

From someone without credentials who uses a reasonable tone, cites evidence and does nothing that sets off warning bells, the surprising claim makes us think this is an independent-thinking individual, a leader—someone who deserves attention.

Surrounded by other credibility-building ingredients, counter-intuitiveness persuades.

☙ ❧

Action Steps

✦ Make a list of surprising claims you're already know you're making. If challenged, which can you convincingly support? Star those; cross out the others.

✦ List accepted truths in your field of work—believed by clients or by other experts. Which do you disagree with and have good backing for doing so?

✦ Find a directory of popular sayings and proverbs and identify some related to your work that you disagree with, such as "haste makes waste" or "better safe than sorry." Again identify which claims you can defend.

✦ Figure out how you can feature your surprising statements in publicity and marketing materials.

The Power of Suspense

Who did it? Who really won? Suspense keeps us tuned to thrillers and crazy elections, and it works in marketing, too.

Nintendo used it to gross $500 million on the best-selling video game up to that point. They planted rumors in schoolyards that an update of Super Mario Brothers was in the works. Then, in the kids' feature movie "The Wizard," the main characters dueled at a video-game tournament in the never-before-seen Version 3. Moviegoers called their pals to report on the characters' new powers and challenges, and whammo—the game flew out of stores in record-breaking numbers.

Selchow & Righter also used suspense to introduce a new game for grownups. Before a key trade show, they sent mailings to toy buyers—first a stylized card with questions on one side, answers on the other. Then a second matching card arrived with different questions and answers. After the third card, which identified the game, their booth was mobbed at the show, with an unprecedented number of orders for Trivial Pursuit.

Tantalize, hold back a detail or item and capitalize on keen anticipation.

On a Lighter Note

"Even cowards can endure hardship; only the brave can endure suspense."

— Mignon McLaughlin

Get Them Involved

Ever try to send in a sweepstakes entry and discover you first have to find certain stamps, detach them and stick them on a specific place? Marketers call such techniques "involvement devices" and advise that the reader's cooperation with such requests not only lengthens the time spent with the promotion but also increases purchases.

Whether on paper or on the web, you can use your creativity to increase readers' involvement. For example:

✦ Ask readers to check off which of several factors apply to them, then add up their score and see what it means.

✦ Provide a space for readers to write down their problems, questions or reasons for wanting something.

✦ If you're raising funds or advocating a cause, ask supporters to sign a petition.

✦ Have readers answer a set of questions, then receive appropriate product recommendations.

✦ Invite readers to test their knowledge and find out whether they really know as much as they think they do.

✦ Provide a customized crossword, brainteaser or word search puzzle that relates to your area of expertise.

Action Steps

✦ Find out how long visitors to your web site typically spend on a key entry page of the site. Add one or more of the involvement devices above. Determine whether or not that lengthens the time they linger on the site, so this in turn increases sales, inquiries or opt-ins.

✦ Add a quiz, checklist, petition or puzzle to a printed promotional piece you've previously used and measure whether or not it increases the response.

The Point, Please!

"It's long and I didn't listen all the way to the end, but it makes some good points," said a colleague in recommending an online video.

Another self-indulgent ramble, I thought, and didn't even go have a look.

Unless you're settling down with a novel or movie, who has time these days for communications that don't stay on point?

To be crisp and concise:

+ Start strongly. Rix Quinn's excellent book *Words That Stick* offers 60 ways to captivate the reader from your first sentence.
+ Minimize background. You don't need a song and dance on where, why, or when the video recommendation that I led with occurred.

- ✦ Stay relevant. If I digressed here about my cat, car or caboose, you'd rightly stop reading.
- ✦ Move along. Quinn suggests improving a draft by reading it out loud. Listen for where you go on too long and cut without mercy. (Edit videos this way, too.)
- ✦ End with a twist. Either tie your topic together with a summary or snap it shut with a surprise that continues to crackle in the mind.

Action Steps

- ✦ Sit down with the printout of a sales letter, newsletter or article and a red pen. Does it start off with a bang? If not, find another section of the piece that would provide a stronger opening, circle that and draw an arrow moving it to the top.
- ✦ Identify any digressions or unnecessary background and cross out those passages.
- ✦ Read the text out loud and star any sections where momentum lags.
- ✦ Insert the changes you highlighted and smooth any transitions as needed.
- ✦ Reflect on lessons learned about staying on point.

Important But Not Urgent

Time management experts recommend various systems for making sure you tackle and complete important to-do's that have no particular urgency. Suppose, however, that you sell something customers tend to consider in that category?

Planning, crisis prevention, skill improvement and repairs or upgrades, for example, often fall by the wayside as calamities and deadlines hog buyers' attention.

Try these tactics:

+ Detail the long-term savings experienced by acting now.
+ Explain the competitive edge achieved by taking care of what rivals are letting slide.
+ Use news tie-ins, such as new laws or instances reported by the media, to dramatize the problem you solve.

✦ Emphasize the emotional benefit of being able to cross it off their task list.

✦ Connect what you sell with activities that have an appropriate season, such as spring cleaning, back-to-school shopping, new-year goal-setting, etc.

✦ Relate your product or service to a trend people care about and act on, like getting healthy, reducing waste or shopping locally.

✦ Motivate the purchase by creating a one-time deal with a deadline.

Food for Thought

"What is important is seldom urgent and what is urgent is seldom important."

— *Dwight D. Eisenhower*

Use the News

When you read the news, you not only keep up with what's happening in the world, you may come across morsels you can use to spread your message in timely, tantalizing ways.

Reading the "most emailed" articles at NewYorkTimes.com and elsewhere is, I find, especially fruitful. I click on article titles relevant to my interests and those that simply intrigue me.

On Sunday, for example, the headline "He Wants Subjects, Verbs and Objects" presented an interview with Delta Air Lines CEO Richard Anderson, who disparaged Power-Point-style communication in bullet points as lacking the clarity and specificity of complete thoughts.

Immediately two clients came to mind who could usefully quote Anderson: Lynn Gaertner-Johnston, who blogs on business communication at BusinessWritingBlog.

com, and Jean Moroney of ThinkingDirections.com, who like Anderson advocates recording ideas in complete sentences.

A news hook like the Anderson interview adds authority for a point you've made, shines a spotlight on an otherwise mundane topic, and resolves the dilemma of what to write about this week in your newsletter, blog or press releases.

Action Steps

+ Develop a system for saving news items that you run across in print and the ideas they sparked on how to use them.

+ If you get your news by radio or TV, develop a system for jotting down the date, program and news item. Many broadcasts have complete transcripts or program notes posted on the web where you can look up the details of what you heard and check the spelling of names before you pass along the stories.

Expand Your Repertoire of Offers

As merchants quicken their drumbeats for holiday sales, you will soon notice traditional year-end special offers, like "Buy two, get one free," "Complimentary gift wrapping" or "Pay nothing until next year."

There's nothing wrong with these incentives. But you attract more attention from shoppers with imaginative offers that perfectly fit your target market, like:

+ Be among the first 10 to enroll and also enjoy a one-on-one lunch with one of the conference speakers.
+ Through December 20, buy a sweater for your little girl—and receive a matching one for her doll, too.
+ Get five free iPods branded with your company's logo with any service contract longer than six months.
+ If your skiwear order totals more than $2,000, you also receive two nights of lodging for two at the "2010 Travel Weekly Most Romantic Ski Lodge in Vermont."

✦ Order a deluxe business plan and also get a personal introduction to Nevada's top venture capital firm.

Think beyond simple discounts to creative, uniquely motivating bonuses. And yes, bonuses work for the business-to-business crowd as well as for the general public.

Action Steps

✦ Brainstorm possible offers by asking yourself, "What do I have access to that our customers would perceive as exclusive, scarce or uniquely valuable?"

✦ Consider how you might trade appealing bonuses with a complimentary, non-competing business.

✦ Ponder ways to increase perceived value by personalizing or upgrading a product or service for those who act quickly or place large orders.

Narrow Their Options

When your childhood toothpaste brand presents you with "Tartar Protection," "Sensitivity Protection," "Cavity Protection" and 14 other versions, it's easy to conclude that more choice is better.

However, two studies by Columbia University psychologist Sheena Iyengar contradict this. When researchers invited gourmet food shoppers to try samples of exotic jams, only 3 percent of those who tried one of 24 varieties purchased a jar, while of those who tried one of just six varieties, 30 percent purchased.

Likewise, when Iyengar compared employee participation in 401(k) pension plans at almost 1,000 companies, she found that as the number of mutual funds offered in a plan rose, the rate of employee participation fell.

Present too many options and people balk.

This explains the wisdom of certain marketing strategies:

+ The effective direct mail letter asks the reader to take one action, not choose among five.
+ Special offers should highlight a deal on one product, not provide a discount on anything in the store.
+ Pointing different types of customers toward their best option not only makes buying easier but also reduces buyer's remorse.

Action Steps

+ Review your direct mail and email pitches to see whether you provided too many options. If so, revise them with just one or two options and try them again.
+ Create recommendation guides: If you're an X, then buy a Y; if you're a G, buy an H. Post these on the web, and train people who answer the phone to use them to guide those who call with questions.

The Literary Agent Reversal

Ever tried to simply hire a literary agent? Usually you can't. The literary agent must first like your book project and believe you have what it takes to be a successful author. You have to persuade the agent to choose you, rather than the reverse.

Even if your industry doesn't normally work this way, you can implement similar selectivity to cultivate an elite image that stands the usual customer/vendor dynamic on its head.

Using Google, I found chiropractors, real estate agents, dentists, veterinarians, stockbrokers and designers who use such selectivity. If you simply call to make an appointment, you can't: "Sorry, we only accept new clients referred by existing clients."

Or set the bar higher by specifying criteria customers must have before you'll do business with them. These might involve objective qualities like income (high or low), environmental friendliness or severity of case (only routine or only challenging), or subjective qualities like needing to "click."

On my web site, for years I had a box headlined, "Will Marcia Yudkin take on your project? Maybe, maybe not..." New clients told me this galvanized them to contact me.

Food for Thought

"Exclusivity and uniqueness are most critical to wealthy consumers. Having too many stores can take away from exclusivity."

— *Milton Pedraza*

No More Rejection!

Once at the outset of a writing workshop, when I asked participants what they most wanted to learn that day, one woman replied, "how never to get another rejection letter."

I replied, "That's easy! Go into another business. All writers receive no-thank-you's."

According to Ari Galper of UnlocktheGame.com, however, that woman could indeed say goodbye to rejections, simply by changing her mindset.

Traditionally, rejection is seen as a normal part of selling, he explains. You play a numbers game—call a lot of people, get rejected by most and accepted by a few. To eliminate rejection, decide that you're looking for the right people to work with. With that attitude, when someone tells you no, you easily go on to the next possibility.

"We've been taught to go for a 'yes,' and that approach triggers a shutdown in the other person," Galper says. "When someone says no and it's not a response to an aggressive request, you've discovered there's not a good fit, that's all. Without a 'push and pull' dynamic between seller and prospect, you sell more."

⤳ ⤶

On a Lighter Note

"Puberty is a phase. Fifteen years of rejection is a lifestyle."

— *Sex and the City*

To Persuade, Prepare

When *Marketing Minute* subscriber Bonnie Neubauer makes telephone calls on behalf of companies, she follows the old Scout motto: Be prepared.

"I read all the literature for the job at hand, making note of the lingo (and definitions so I use it correctly). Then I ask those in charge of the specifics, #1, What objections are you getting? and #2, Which selling points are exciting clients? For each objection, I list responses to overcome them. #2 indicates the hook I might use to start the call.

"Then I write a script and read it aloud until it sounds totally natural. On a separate sheet of paper, I write the key words from each paragraph one per line, in the order I'll present them. At the very bottom in big print is the goal of each call. Finally I crumple up the script and toss it out.

"I place all the supporting literature, including objection lists and vocabulary words, around my desk, sit with good posture and smile. Only then do I make the call."

Prepared, Bonnie sounds unscripted and persuasive. Results follow.

Action Steps

+ Rehearse an important pitch by role playing with a friend. Ask your friend to take on the attitude your audience might have—resistant, skeptical, distracted, impatient or belligerent—and then provide feedback afterwards.

+ Prepare by practicing in front of your dog, cat or goldfish.

Be Yourself–Dressed Up

A *Fast Company* magazine article on the hows and whys of "authenticity" in marketing teems with paradoxes. For example, Juan Valdez, the long-time poster boy for Colombian coffee, is praised for being "humble but uncompromising, dedicated to the hard work of raising coffee by hand." Yet there's no such person. The mustached, poncho-wearing Juan Valdez we see in ads is an actor from New York City.

Small businesses and solo practices have a much easier time turning authenticity to their advantage than corporations like Samuel Adams beer (supposedly from Boston but mainly brewed in Cincinnati).

Authenticity doesn't mean showing yourself exactly as you are, spotlighting all your flaws and talents. It means selecting and dramatizing something that's true and perceived as advantageous by your target audience.

Weaknesses can be part of authenticity as long as the overall image impresses. Negatives also become positives in another context. For instance, I sometimes call myself "unemployable," a horrible thing if I were trying to get a job, but for an independent consultant, it becomes a humorous way to highlight honesty and candor.

Action Steps

+ Within your industry or occupation, identify individuals or companies that you admire and that come across as authentic. Analyze what they do to create that impression and how you might use them as a role model.

+ Do you practice what you preach? If not, that detracts from your authenticity. Give yourself an audit of how well you're living up to your stated principles and make changes accordingly.

+ Consider whether you've ever gone too far in the pursuit of authenticity, to the point where you bared flaws that damaged your reputation. Correct such overreaching if you can.

Your Address Sends a Message

Fairly or not, your business address communicates a message just as do your choice of clothes and the car you drive. What does your business address say?

A few years ago, interior designer Treena Crochet got tired of hearing "Where's Hingham?" when people looked at her business card. (It's on Boston's South Shore.) Then she heard me mention why I'd kept a Boston address and phone number after moving outside of the city: Location in a well-known city seems more substantial than in a little-known town. Treena immediately put down a deposit for a private mailbox service on Newbury Street in Boston and reaped a disproportionate reward.

"Now people across the country take notice that I am from Boston," she says. "In the design business, it's all about image. On the lecture circuit it's about credibility. Companies that sponsor my seminars react favorably that I'm based in Boston. Locally, people look at my card and say 'Newbury Street, nice!'" (Newbury Street hosts the Ritz-Carlton Hotel and many high-prestige boutiques and galleries.) "The validation is more than worth any practical inconvenience."

❧ ❧

On a Lighter Note

"Most of us can read the writing on the wall; we just assume it's addressed to someone else."

— *Ivern Ball*

Part 5
Approaches That Can Backfire

The Fly in the Offer

Twice recently, I felt tempted to seize upon a well-known marketer's special offer. The first promotion said $798.89 in bonuses accompanied a free trial. It turned out, however, that the trial cost $19.95—"for shipping." Although $19.95 still made it a great deal, my enthusiasm vanished.

The second promotion described a 30-day trial that cost nothing up front, except that you had to cancel "by telephone" before the 30 days were up or your credit card would be charged. At this, my mind started racing, guessing that the number would be constantly busy, or hidden someplace only a genius could find. And in fact, the number to call to cancel the order was not provided prior to or on the order form.

Both offers ran afoul of the psychology of today's consumers. People are skeptical. No one wants to be taken for a fool. So we are quick to see signs of trickery where perhaps none were intended.

Instead, earn the trust of your market by accurately and fully disclosing the terms of the deal, with no snags, no fine print.

❧ ❦

Action Steps

+ Imagine that the government has passed a law for companies in your industry that says, "No fine print allowed." What steps would you need to take to comply? And why not be up front without such a mandate?

+ Examine your marketing documents for non-disclosure of shipping costs, guarantees with subtle catches, semi-hidden disclaimers, language that was written purposely to be misleading, policies designed to stonewall complaints, etc. Now suppose that you had to defend these terms on national TV. Could you do so with a straight face and heartfelt conviction? If not, eliminate or change the fine print now.

Should You Exaggerate?

In my local paper, a house-for-sale description gets me shaking my head. "Fifteen minutes to ___," says the ad. Come on: It's fifteen miles along a windy road whose speed limit is 45 miles per hour with a stretch of 25 miles per hour through a village with a well-known speed trap.

I have the same reaction reading an automatically generated follow-up message from the president of the shopping-cart company whose product I signed up for. "Set it up in minutes," he says. Really? I spent more than two hours working my way through the options and still hadn't reached the point of testing it.

In your enthusiasm to promote the virtues of what you're selling, it's tempting to put a sunnier face on the facts than you would in a courtroom. According to extensive global research by the Whole Brain Corporation, however, 44 percent of adults consider truth more important than passion, while

28 percent respond mainly to emotional overtones (the remainder have a mixed orientation).

Exaggerating something your customers may already know or will soon probably experience for themselves is especially foolhardy.

Food for Thought

"Truth is such a rare thing, it is delightful to tell it."

— *Emily Dickinson*

Be Believable

O h, come on!"

That was my reaction on reading this, in the second paragraph of a full-page magazine ad: "[Company name] is virtually the only franchise brand committed to providing genuinely nutritious and delicious products."

This couldn't be true, I thought.

When you make a preposterous claim, it taints everything else you say. Am I willing to let that statement pass and believe that this company's food is low-calorie, gluten-free and full of probiotics? No.

In marketing, it can be worse to say something unbelievable than something untrue.

If you have a claim that's hard to believe, simply saying it doesn't convince. You must either explain how it's true, provide third-party proof or back-pedal it to a more believable statement.

Don't expect weasel words like "virtually" to bail you out with a skeptical reader.

To check my instinctive response, before writing this piece I searched Google for "healthy food franchise." As I'd suspected, dozens of companies show up in that category.

"One of America's fastest growing new brands" (so they say) is rapidly shooting itself in the foot.

Action Steps

✦ Invite three or four friends out to lunch and hand them a copy of an ad, brochure or web page of yours. Ask them to pretend they are a typical business reader and then identify anything in the document that they do not believe. If their findings surprise you, ponder this discussion further when you get back to the office.

✦ Select sentences from your marketing materials that attempt to make a convincing point. Practice changing each sentence so as to make it more believable and then less believable. Which of these versions is most consistent with your ethics and desired professional image?

Don't Reject Questions

Yesterday I ran across this in an interview with a veteran marketer: "If you think that buying my $2000 product lets you ask me questions, that's not a reasonable expectation."

Wow.

Most people expect that if they're just thinking about buying a $2000 product, they have a right to ask questions. And you should indulge this expectation whenever possible.

When you answer questions, much more is going on than just giving out information.

+ You can demonstrate courtesy, respect and responsiveness.
+ People get a chance to gauge whether they'd enjoy doing business with you.
+ You take on the dimensions of a real person, not a mere name, title or icon.

✦ You can show a depth of knowledge, wisdom or common sense.

✦ Listeners trust you more.

More often than not, and whether they consciously realize it or not, when people ask questions they are as interested in those elements as they are in the content of your answer.

So if you don't already have a forum through which you can encourage questions, maybe it's time to create one.

Action Steps

✦ Count how many ways you have established for people considering a purchase to ask you questions: By email, phone, fax, a contact form on your web site (which actually prompts responses, we hope), live chat on the site, Twitter, Linked In, comments on your blog, etc. Add one more communication channel if you can.

✦ Now audit how you or your staff answer people's questions. Are you respectful, helpful, pleasant and fully forthcoming—or impatient and brusque?

Incentives and Identity

In an Amazon bestseller campaign, the author of a new book persuades friends, colleagues and strangers to provide giveaways that someone who buys the book on one certain day will receive. Then the author persuades as many buddies as possible to pitch their subscribers on buying the book and bonuses that day.

A story cited in a terrific book on marketing, *Made to Stick,* provides one reason why this technique bothers me so much.

To promote an educational film on fire safety, legendary adman John Caples asked firefighters whether they preferred an electric popcorn popper or a set of chef's knives as a reward for reviewing the film. They responded angrily: "You think we'd adopt a fire safety program because of some #$&%! popcorn popper?"

The reward violated the firefighters' sense of identity, the book explains.

Likewise, to me, an author and lifelong book lover, writing is a noble calling and books treasured objects. Offering incentives worth $499 for a $19.95 book purchased only next Tuesday clashes with those commitments.

I always say no to bestseller campaigns, but others may not feel the conflict.

Action Steps

+ The next time you're considering bonuses, don't make assumptions about what can serve as an effective incentive to buy now. Ask your target market. Test various possibilities—including no added incentive and one that goes to charity.

+ The strongest incentive may be something that can't normally be purchased or obtained at all, such as access or recognition. Brainstorm way outside the box instead of piling on more of what everyone else offers, when you're considering bonuses.

Latest = Greatest?

Clients often ask me what I think of just-invented marketing tactics touted as the ticket to quick riches. "Completely wrong for your blue-collar, 50+ market," I told one. For another, the verdict was "Great idea, but first collect or create products you can sell to respondents. Only then should you generate colossal traffic."

Whether innovative or traditional, effective marketing requires attention to fundamentals you can easily overlook in your fascination with what's new.

- ✦ Will a marketing medium appeal to the customers who best match your product or service? The age 40+ business owners and organizational marketers who comprise my core clientele, for instance, don't spend their time looking for cute downloadable videos.
- ✦ Have you laid the groundwork for success to pay off? Focusing on related offerings for a single market

outperforms developing each grand idea you fall in love with.

✦ Have you chosen an angle that promises what customers want? Products solving problems that prospects know they have do better than those pitched as beneficial in deeper but less familiar ways.

By itself, cutting-edge doesn't always cut it.

Action Steps

✦ Develop a checklist of additional criteria that can help you judge whether or not a cool new marketing tactic is worth your time and effort.

✦ Create a sandbox in which you can play around with cutting-edge new techniques outside of your primary business. Then when it's appropriate, apply what you've learned for your regular customer base.

Show Your Heart?

Gary Hirshberg had no advertising budget when he helped launch what is today's largest organic yogurt company, Stonyfield Farm. So he ran environmental awareness messages on container lids, urging action on global warming, public transportation and so on. "I got a 26 percent growth rate by showing my emotions on my lids," he says.

Guessing organic food buyers would appreciate a commitment to a healthier planet was a pretty safe bet.

Some linkages of businesses with causes aren't as wise. Before your business publicly supports a cause, use this checklist.

+ Is the information you're spreading reliable? You don't want to have to run a retraction next week because you embraced a hoax or a "charity" that's actually a con game. Do research. Look for trustworthy third-party endorsements.

✦ Is the cause uncontroversial? Don't judge this by friends' and neighbors' allegiances. If an "anti" side of the story exists, some customers or business partners of yours may belong to the opposite camp.

✦ Is the tone the cause takes consistent with your image? A strident, militant campaign clashes with an organization trying to project compassion.

Food for Thought

"I do my bit to improve the world, but I think it's very important to get things done on the quiet. I'm sick to death of famous people standing up and using their celebrity to promote a cause."

— *Russell Crowe*

Beware Secondary Passions

A neighbor asked me about a local talk I'd attended on forest foraging. "Was the speaker any—"

I quickly shook my head. "His content was fine, until he started talking about how aliens are leaving us signs that we have to do a better job taking care of the earth."

"Oh! We were thinking of hiring him for an event this summer." Steve gave me a rueful smile. "I guess not."

The incident reminded me of a business book I was planning to recommend, until I reached the appendix, in which the author evangelized for an offbeat cause that was completely irrelevant to the book.

"Why did you include that sermon?" I wrote the author. "It makes you look unprofessional. It casts a cloud of suspicion over the rest of what you wrote."

"I strongly disagree," he replied. "You picked up a book about small business marketing and got exposed to ideas that can save lives. Because I self-publish, I have a platform for spreading awareness."

I understand the temptation. But what is desperately important to you can drastically undermine your perceived expertise.

❧ ❦

Action Steps

+ Do you have a cherished cause or two? Convene a council of friends or colleagues whom you can trust to be honest and ask them to rate the causes' "kook quotient": On a scale of 1 to 10, are they very harmless or cute (1) or extremely weird and even a bit scary (10)? The higher your score, the more cautious you need to be about promoting your cause in conjunction with your business.

+ Obtain the same kind of ratings for your hobbies and let them guide you on whether or not to mention them to business reporters and in your business bio.

The "One Up" Factor

Once I was talking with my editor at a public radio station when she got beeped. She said, "Sorry, I'll need to call you back. There's a call from the White House."

That's a story I can tell in some settings and not others. To some audiences, this story raises my status, putting me three steps removed from the President of the United States. To other audiences, it makes me seem full of myself and they'll like me less.

Where are you acting "one up," and does it help or hurt you?

My dentist's appointment card includes a notice of a $25 no-show/late cancellation fee that irritates the heck out of me because I get no apology when I arrive on time and wait half an hour for service. The message communicated: Our time is valuable; yours isn't.

Similarly, you may have received automatic email messages like, "Thanks for your message, I'll get back to you when I can as I'm concentrating on urgent projects." That's disrespectful, a colleague complains, conveying: "What I'm doing now is more important than you."

∼ ∽

Food for Thought

"'The question is,' said Humpty Dumpty, 'which is to be master—that's all.'"

— *Lewis Carroll,* Through the Looking Glass

Part 6
Pricing Psychology

Consider Posting Your Service Prices

California adman Hal Pawluk found himself telling a familiar story: My web site's up, but isn't generating business. What's wrong?

Pawluk tried a surprising tactic: He listed his prices, high ones. Four months later, he reeled in a $1.2 million dollar client. More recently, the web site brought him several multi-million-dollar leads.

"After I posted prices, requests for freebies completely stopped," he reports. "Visitors who think, 'Sounds too good, can't really be this good'—now my prices implicitly tell them others have paid a premium price for my services. And the ones who think, 'Sounds great, but I couldn't possibly afford him' now can make a rational business decision about whether or not hiring me would be a good move."

Pawluk adds, "Now when someone reaches me I know they're a serious lead and worth pursuing diligently, and I spend almost no time chasing dead ends."

Occasionally a small, strategic change in one's marketing approach produces an enormous payoff.

Action Steps

+ Reflect on recent email and phone exchanges with prospective clients. What percentage of these prospects seem to take themselves out of the running of doing business with you because of price? If it's more than 50 percent, follow Pawluk's lead and post your prices. This will probably save you lots of time and energy.

+ For a more formal test, during the next calendar month keep track of how many inquiries you receive and how many go-aheads. During the calendar month after that, post your prices on your web site if you were not doing so, or take them down if you were posting them. Again keep track of your inquiries and go-aheads. Draw tentative conclusions about whether posted prices help or hurt you.

How to Pull Off Higher Prices

What is your work worth?

In her book, *How to Survive & Prosper as an Artist*, Caroll Michels tells the story of two artists. One had worked full-time as an artist for more than 20 years, was represented by prestigious galleries and had received grants and media recognition. She priced her paintings at $5,000 to $7,500 each.

Another artist, a real estate agent who painted on the side, had never had an exhibition before or won awards of any sort. Yet she arranged to hang her paintings at her local public library and sold them for up to $6,000 each.

Why did the second artist, a beginner, get as much money for her work as the veteran artist?

Because she asked.

Before you protest that this dynamic couldn't work for you, give it a shot. Try sitting up straight and confidently claiming that you're worth more than the going rate. They won't cough up extra money for you every time—but when you believe it, they're persuaded too, much more often than if you meekly accept the usual price.

❧ ❧

Action Steps

✦ Convene a panel of friends or business associates, and while facing them, tell them in a simple declarative sentence how much you charge. Ask for their honest feedback: Did you come across as confident? Did they believe you are worth what you charge, from the way you said it?

✦ List all the reasons you can think of why you can't or shouldn't or don't want to charge double what you currently charge. For each reason, imagine what the gutsy real estate agent turned artist in Caroll Michels' story would say in response. If she is not convincing you, imagine her calling in five other business-minded artists to help argue with you. Consider how you feel about your prices now.

Stay Firm on Your Fees

If a hot potential client pleads poverty, should you lower your fee?

Dan Kennedy, a street-smart marketer with decades of experience, confesses that he recently fell for such an appeal from a startup. After he'd uncharacteristically agreed to defer his fee, he learned that this supposedly cash-poor operation had just paid some $15,000 to a naming firm and $15,000 for a logo.

"Regardless of how fervently they deny it, people always have and will come up with whatever money is necessary to get whatever they really want," Kennedy reflected ruefully. "Never alter your price or terms in response."

I had a similar experience with a client who said she could hardly pay anything for publicity help. I gave her a rock-bottom estimate, and when she didn't hire me, I figured she couldn't afford even that. Six months later she showed me clips she'd gotten in major media—through the help of a $3,000+ a month firm, whom she'd hired for several months.

Stay firm on your fee, and you won't be haunted by regrets.

Food for Thought

"The moment you make a mistake in pricing, you're eating into your reputation or your profits."

— *Katharine Paine*

Pricing You Can Live With

I went to 60-minute sessions rather than 45 minutes because it's not good for clients if I have to rush," a *Marketing Minute* subscriber who's a therapist told me. "Clients with insurance pay me themselves for the extra quarter hour. This way, I don't resent how little the managed care programs reimburse me or how little therapeutic time those programs want me to have."

The resentment factor is usually overlooked as an element of wise pricing, but I've seen it sabotage client relationships and consume emotional energy better spent elsewhere. Charge too little and you may find yourself short-tempered with clients and complaining inappropriately to colleagues. You might even short-change the client and have to re-do the work or provide a refund.

When setting your fees, ask yourself whether you can live with receiving that amount. If not, charge more.

Whether you're an attorney trying to keep people out of jail or a designer creating a graphic image for a business, clients deserve to have your whole mind on their work—and so do you.

ð   ñ

Action Steps

+ Reflect on the client behaviors and situations that trigger complaints from you and your staff. Can you do a better job of setting up expectations and boundaries so those annoyances do not occur? Imagine raising your fees to the point where what bothered you no longer does. That's what you need to charge to eliminate resentment.

+ Count the number or percentage of dissatisfied clients in the last year. Ask yourself whether you delivered less value than they had a right to expect. Would you have done what was needed to satisfy them if you'd charged more? If so, it's time to raise your fees.

Some Pricing Principles

How attentive to prices were you during the holiday shopping season that just passed? No matter how sophisticated you think you are, certain pricing factors influence you—and your customers or clients—according to research. Take note of these facts in pricing your products or services:

✦ Two-tier pricing, with regular and deluxe options, adds to revenues not only from the higher-priced product or service, but also from increased sales of the regular version. The higher tier boosts the perceived value of the lower-priced option.

✦ To stimulate sales without devaluing your image, offer time-specific rebates or discounts with an explicit rationale rather than lower prices across the board.

✦ Set a high price by comparing your item to something buyers know costs more. For instance, compare audio recordings to the cost of live seminars rather than books; software to the cost of custom programming; consulting to the cost of hiring an expert on staff. This works!

✦ In a market where many customers shop by price, there are always others willing to pay premium prices for extra value: faster delivery, guaranteed return phone calls, training or advice included in the price or a bundling of products and services not available elsewhere.

On a Lighter Note

"The disparity between a restaurant's price and food quality rises in direct proportion to the size of the pepper mill."

— *Bryan Miller*

Offer Pricing Options

L ast week's heavy snowstorms in Boston reminded me of a winter when we got so much snow the plowing service told us, "One more storm and we won't be able to plow your driveway again—there's no place to put more snow."

Shortly afterwards our landlord dropped by complaining about his bad luck. Given the option of paying per plowing session or for the whole season, he'd chosen the per piece method, betting we'd have a mild winter. "No more storms, please. I'm getting killed!" he said. If most customers chose the other option, the plowing service would be buried financially. Even so, the service was smart to place the choice at the customer's doorstep.

There's a marketing lesson here: Some prefer to pay according to what they actually receive, while others like knowing exactly how much they'll pay, no matter what. Buyers guess their anticipated usage, but if they turn out to be wrong, most accept the consequences.

When the economic climate is cloudy, giving customers more than one type of service plan helps them feel in control.

≈ ≈

Action Steps

+ Try to remember instances in which an actual or prospective customer complained that the basis for your pricing was unfair. Would they have been satisfied with a different method of arriving at the price? If so, could you offer that alternative as an option for customers?

+ Research how other industries that are quite different from yours charge—such as gyms, heating fuel, legal services, office supplies, pool cleaning, cosmetics. Are any of their pricing schemes such that you and your clientele might both be amenable to charging that way? Run a test with a limited portion of your customer base.

Mental Mistakes About Pricing

Do you set your prices according to what you believe your market can afford?

If you're a professional, do you offer a sliding scale for payment?

When anyone requests a price break, do you automatically agree?

All of the above practices carry a danger that can needlessly keep your revenues down. When you're tempted to set low prices, remember these points:

✦ What someone can afford and what they will pay aren't necessarily related in any logical or predictable way. I've had clients hire me who had next to no income or savings, while someone with a Fortune 100-sized budget decides the same offering costs too much.

✦ Someone may ask for or expect a bargain but end up paying the original fee.

✦ What you say about your products and services and how you present your company and conduct yourself each influence what folks will pay.

✦ Those willing to pay more may be the most loyal, trouble-free clients to work with.

Test your prices, instead of making assumptions about what your customers can afford!

Action Steps

✦ If you're in a business where you're constantly giving clients project quotes, create a checklist for creating those quotes that includes as the final step: Wipe out any assumptions. Do not make assumptions about what the client can afford or is willing to pay.

✦ Find companies that charge significantly more than you do for similar products or services. Analyze why you think they succeed with higher prices. Determine the likely costs and benefits of raising your prices to match theirs.

Pricing Psychology Quirks

When is one dollar not one dollar? The field of behavioral economics offers psychological insights on how people perceive and act on pricing offers.

+ Presentation order matters. People are more likely to buy a $10 item if you show it after $100 and $1,000 items than before. Always show the most expensive option first.

+ People love windfalls. Offers have greater appeal when you promise additional items of a different type as extras than when bundling the same items into a single package.

+ People love savings. When you call attention to the amount of a discount, customers focus on that amount as earnings rather than think about what they spent.

✦ People hate surprises. When customers expect to pay $21 and do, they're much happier than when they expect to pay $20 and encounter a charge of $21.

✦ People dislike separate charges. It hurts more to pay $50 plus $120 plus $75 than $245. If you can then arrange for that $245 to be deducted automatically from expected income, as from paychecks or tax refunds, the payment psychologically disappears.

On a Lighter Note

"A vacation is a sunburn at premium prices."

— *Hal Chadwicke*

Take the Pain Out of Prices

A price is a price, right? Not really, according to Cornell University researchers, who tested whether restaurant owners would profit most when menu prices were formatted as $20.00, 20.00 or twenty dollars.

To their surprise, the 20.00 format netted the most, with customers spending 8 percent more when menus used numerals to represent prices, minus any dollar signs.

Without the dollar sign or the word "dollars," diners were apparently reminded least that what they were ordering was making them a tiny bit poorer.

Specialists in the field of "menu engineering" have also discovered that menus bring in more revenue when they insert prices at the end of each small paragraph describing the item, rather than all lined up in a column that can be quickly scanned from top to bottom.

Likewise, those who study these things tell us that we tend to perceive $23 to be less than $23.00.

One more finding: When looking at menus, we take prices like $20.00 as indicative of higher quality food than prices like $19.99.

Action Steps

+ Test the effects of changes in the pricing format of your price list.

+ Test the effects of changes in the font style and type size of your prices, whether on the web or on paper.

+ Test the effects of changes in the sequencing of items in your price list.

+ Test the effects of changes in the color and boldness in which prices appear.

Part 7
Keeping Customers

Eliminate Ordering Obstacles

Imagine coming to a checkout counter, wallet in hand, facing a smiling clerk whose T-shirt says "Don't Trust Me" and who refuses to answer your questions. Bye-bye to that purchase, right?

Much the same happened to me when I went to the web to order a $197 product I'd heard about. I wanted to clarify whether the "videos" I'd get with the product came on DVD or online, but there was no email link or phone number for asking.

Where the site requested my credit-card details, it had no secure-server icon.

It described a money-back guarantee. To invoke it, I'd need to call a certain number...which was not provided.

Doubt piled upon doubt, and I did not order, though I strongly wanted this item.

The product purportedly came from someone who'd sold millions of dollars in products online. If that's true, millions more were lost that would have come through with a more customer-friendly ordering procedure.

Are you obstructing near-sales? Probably. Assume a cautious buyer, and address every question and concern so hesitation cannot get a foothold.

≈ ≈

Action Steps

+ Create a physical or digital file called "ordering obstacles." In it, jot down notes about your experience every time you get confused or frustrated placing an order, either online, in person or by phone. Then use this file as a checklist for your own ordering pages and procedures.

+ Test the usability of an order form by watching someone attempt to order, while providing running commentary out loud on what they're trying to do and encountering. According to Jakob Nielsen, author of *Designing Web Usability,* watching just five users in this way reveals 85 percent of usability problems with your copy and process. Change your order form and test again.

Head Off Buyer's Remorse

You'd be hard put to find a person in the industrialized world who hasn't wondered about the wisdom of a purchase in the cold light of the next day. Psychologists and sales experts call this widespread phenomenon "buyer's remorse."

Take these steps to soothe that anxiety instead of letting it blossom into a refund request.

- Send a personal thank-you to each buyer when possible—not an obviously canned autoresponder message or a mass-produced cover letter, but a brief one-to-one note. A personal touch reduces fear that you were just out to take their money.
- Deliver everything you promised, and more. Adding an unannounced "extra" sparks delight that helps buyers relax.
- Remind purchasers of the benefits they're going to enjoy from your product or service. Give them clear

instructions for anything they must do next so that they have a positive experience using what they bought.

+ Invite buyers to contact you if they have any questions, problems or compliments. Most won't, but your offer further defuses any worry on their part.

Action Steps

+ Reduce buyer's remorse by tinkering with your guarantee. (Sometimes people request refunds more out of anxiety over the impending end of the guarantee period than out of dissatisfaction.) Change the length and the wording and watch what happens to your refund rate.

+ Brainstorm 10 ways you can increase the extent to which customers feel like they've bought from a trustworthy friend. Put at least two of these ideas into action.

Should You Guilt-Trip Customers?

R ead marketing guarantees carefully, and you'll see an increasing number of people saying something like "And if you're not happy for any reason, I'll refund what you paid out of my own pocket."

By using the phrase "out of my own pocket," the theory runs, you're reminding customers that their refund deprives you—personally—of revenue.

When I heard that, I wanted to wash out my ears. Yuck!

Instead, to increase satisfaction and raise your "stick" rate:

- ✦ Provide an extra with each shipment—an unexpected little gift.
- ✦ Enclose a handwritten note with each product, even just a sticky note saying "Thanks for your order" or "Enjoy!"

- ✦ Include a cover letter that describes how to get started using the purchase, so the customer doesn't feel confused, regretful or overwhelmed.
- ✦ Overdeliver on quality.
- ✦ Arrange for fast delivery.
- ✦ Ensure the closest possible match between product descriptions and what customers receive.
- ✦ Describe how the customer can get any questions answered.

Think "feel good" rather than "feel guilty." Make customers happy and taken care of, and your pockets stay full.

On a Lighter Note

"Pack your bags, we're going on a guilt trip."

— *Jimmy Buffett*

Your Client's Inner Child

Don't be surprised if your client's childhood experiences sneak out during adult business transactions.

Years ago when I edited a Harvard professor's business plan, she said she couldn't bear seeing corrections in red ink. Could I use any other color than the one that brought back unpleasant experiences from school days?

When I ask grownups graduating from one of my training programs if they'd like a framable certificate marking the event, they always chuckle and say yes. Receiving a diploma and a title, such as Certified Web Site Makeover Consultant, brings a childlike experience of pride.

Occasionally I've had site review clients say they felt hurt that I didn't like their site. You'd think someone who says their web site isn't working and pays to find out why would expect some negative comments.

And recently when a *Marketing Minute* subscriber castigated me in highly emotional terms, I took her off the list and then got accused of acting like a spoiled brat. I thought I was being mature: Who needs this? But maybe that *was* the child in me striking back.

~ ~

Action Steps

+ Think back to the high drama of your junior high school years. Remember incidents that involved jealousy, obsessions, cruelty, anger, greed, high jinks and revenge. Now imagine paler adult versions of those incidents. Are any bells ringing?

+ List as many ways of pleasing five-to-eight-year-olds as you can. Then go back through your list, asking yourself which of them can be adapted to appeal to the inner child of your adult clients.

Tossing in a Lagniappe

In New Orleans they call it a "lagniappe"—an extra pastry tossed in with your order. At bakery shops elsewhere, they call it a "baker's dozen"—thirteen instead of twelve cupcakes or donuts. It's a very cheap way to purchase customer loyalty, and it works even if you don't sell edible goods.

Marketing Minute subscriber Lisa Stone, president of Fit for 2, Inc., experienced this effect with Webvan, from whom she ordered most of her groceries. Postage rates had just gone up in the U.S., and Webvan slipped 20 one-cent stamps into her grocery order that week as a gift.

"I really appreciated not having to stand in the long post office lines to get those stamps," Stone says. "Webvan saved me time and aggravation." And as an online grocery delivery company, isn't that their reason for being?

"It cost them only 20 cents but it earned them much more than that in my book," says Stone. "Marketing campaigns don't have to involve expensive giveaways." What can you give your customers that costs little and means a lot?

❧   ❧

Food for Thought

"If you're a small business, maybe you can't compete on size or price, but you have to compete on customer service."

— *Chris Denove*

What's Next?

Ever finish listening to or reading something and feel jazzed to buy something that takes you farther on the same learning path?

This happened to me twice in recent weeks. The first time, I scoured the catalog and site of an audio publisher, trying in vain to identify the logical next product after the one I'd found electrifying. There had been a sticky note saying "Start here!" when I opened the audio binder, but no counterpart note at the end.

The second time, 100 pages into a book I was greatly enjoying, I figured there must be dialogues or informal teaching available from the organization founded by the author, who'd died. My initial 20-minute search turned up nothing, although in a second search this morning, I found what I was looking for, hidden deep within the site.

Don't make enthusiasts work so hard to continue to their next step.

Include "If you liked X, then get Y" notes on your site. Or say so in a cover letter shipped with the product or in a follow-up email or postcard.

❧ ❧

Action Steps

+ Create a two-column grid. In the left column, list your major products or services. Across from each one, in the right column, identify another product or service of yours that customers would logically need next. Then identify one or more ways to communicate the next step to your buyers.

+ Return to your two-column grid and for each coupling of what someone bought and its next step, write down the ideal timing for you to communicate the next logical step. Would that be immediately after purchase, upon delivery of the goods, a week after delivery or a month after purchase? Now make plans for implementation of your "what's next" add-ons.

Want Fries With That?

While moving around boxes in my office yesterday, I found leftover copies of my last company brochure. Given the increased convenience and efficiency of web sites, I haven't urgently needed to update and reprint the brochure. But that leaves a gaping hole in my sales process. When someone orders printed books from me, they should receive the printed equivalent of McDonald's' "Want Fries With That?"

Someone who just purchased—or who just received a tangible item they bought online—is highly likely to buy related items if you prompt them, make the additional purchase easy and provide an appealing offer.

If you sell online, you can program an upsell offer into the shopping cart so that someone who buys item A sees the question, "Would you like Related Item A or B with that?" You can also insert an upsell offer on the "Thank You" page that buyers see after completing the purchase and on the page people see after subscribing to your ezine.

If you sell tangible products, tuck a product brochure, sales letter or discount flyer into the package or shopping bag. I will!

❧ ☙

Action Steps

✦ This week, notice all the upsells that cross your path— in restaurants, when you call to order office supplies, as you donate to charities or on the web while you sign up for a free newsletter. Take notes on wording that sounds natural and feels helpful, and decide on wording for upsells that will fit your business.

✦ If you've decided on a spoken upsell, practice your up-sell spiel with a friend until your friend declares you ready for prime time.

✦ If you've decided on a written upsell, put tracking in place so you can easily compare the before-and-after results of your upsell. Then test it.

Each Customer is Unique

Everyone wants to be treated as one of a kind, says Jay Conrad Levinson, who has edified readers in 39 languages with his "Guerrilla Marketing" series of books. "It is quite difficult but crucial," he says, "to create a human bond with customers," instead of treating them as instances of the demographic groups to which they belong.

For marketers, this means keeping generalizations about your customer base, however solid, to yourself. Never write or say when answering questions or responding to a complaint, "Our typical customer feels such-and-such" or "Everyone else likes this feature." That's irrelevant and sometimes even insulting to someone who doesn't.

It means developing a voice for your marketing that makes you real, while still professional, to your customers, so that they in turn respond as the individuals they are.

It means making personal gestures that show customers they're more than entries on a balance sheet. For Levinson, FedEx's competitive edge comes from the fact that the FedEx driver gives his dog a biscuit.

"The stronger the human bond, the stronger the business bond," says Levinson.

Food for Thought

"People forget that having a customer service transaction is not just about solving a problem, but also about the experience."

— *Amit Shankardass*

Recommended Books

The following books provide valuable insights into marketing psychology. If you can buy or read only one of them, my hands-down suggestion is the first on the list.

✦ Cialdini, Robert, *Influence: The Psychology of Persuasion*. Revised edition. New York: Harper Paperbacks, 2006. A classic, known and quoted by every prominent copywriter I know.

✦ Feig, Barry, *Hot Button Marketing: Push the Emotional Buttons That Get People to Buy*. Avon, MA: Adams Media, 2006. Excellent primer on types of contemporary consumer values.

✦ Goldstein, Noah et al, *Yes! 50 Scientifically Proven Ways to Be Persuasive*. New York: Free Press, 2008. Lively discussion of interesting research studies on marketing persuasion.

✦ Hogan, Kevin, *The Psychology of Persuasion: How to*

Persuade Others to Your Way of Thinking. Gretna, LA: Pelican Publishing Company, 1996. Persuasion using Neuro-Linguistic Programming principles on how the mind works.

✦ Hall, Doug with Jeffrey Stamp, *Meaningful Marketing: 100 Data-Proven Truths and 402 Practical Ideas for Selling More with Less Effort.* Cincinnati: Brain Brew Books, 2003. Outstanding compendium of research-backed marketing principles and their business implications.

✦ Heath, Chip and Heath, Dan, *Made to Stick: Why Some Ideas Survive and Others Die.* New York: Random House, 2007. Journalistic discussion of simplicity, surprise, concreteness, credibility, emotion and stories in marketing.

✦ Sugarman, Joseph, *Triggers: 30 Sales Tools You Can Use to Control the Mind of Your Prospect to Motivate, Influence and Persuade.* Las Vegas, DelStar Books, 1999. Great anecdotes illustrating sound principles.

✦ Whitman, Drew Eric, *Ca$hvertising: How to Use More Than 100 Secrets of Ad-Agency Psychology to Make Big Money Selling Anything to Anyone.* Franklin Lakes, NJ: Career Press, 2009. Extremely practical and reader-friendly.

Get the Whole Series!

What you are reading is the first of five volumes collecting my *Marketing Minute* columns and presenting them by theme. The other volumes are:

- Book 2: *Meatier Marketing Copy: Insights on Copywriting That Generates Leads and Sparks Sales*
- Book 3: *Strategic Marketing: Insights on Setting Smart Directions for Your Business*
- Book 4: *Publicity Tactics: Insights on Creating Lucrative Media Buzz*
- Book 5: *The Marketing Attitude: Insights That Help You Build a Worthy Business*

The series includes two audio CDs for each volume, on which I read the columns in that book as well as bonus columns. Listening to the contents in your car or while exercising often triggers ideas you'll want to implement in your company, professional practice or nonprofit organization.

For more information or to purchase the rest of the Marketing Insight Guides, go to:

www.marketinginsightguides.com.

If you're not already a subscriber, sign up to receive the *Marketing Minute* free in your inbox every Wednesday by going to www.yudkin.com/markmin.htm.

Index

About the Author

Marcia Yudkin launched her writing career in 1981 by persuading an editor at the *New York Times* to publish her article in its first Education Life section.

She has persuaded National Public Radio to broadcast her commentaries, publishers such as Penguin USA, HarperCollins, Henry Holt and Career Press to publish her books, magazines like *The New York Times Magazine, TWA Ambassador, USAir Magazine,* and *Business 2.0* to run her articles, and periodicals including *Success Magazine, Entrepreneur, Working Woman, Women in Business* and the *Boston Globe* to write about her.

Her "Marketing Minute" segment aired weekly throughout New England for more than a year on WABU TV, and it turned into a free weekly newsletter on creative marketing and publicity that reaches more than 12,000 loyal subscribers from all around the world.

Marcia Yudkin serves as a mentor and provides creative marketing ideas to business owners, independent professionals and corporate marketers in industries ranging from business coaching and software publishing to translation firms and local retail stores.

She has a Ph.D. degree from Cornell University and a B.A. from Brown University.

For More Information

Main web site: www.yudkin.com

Subscribe to the *Marketing Minute*: www.yudkin.com/markmin.htm

Mentoring program: www.marketingformore.com

Naming and tag line service: www.namedatlast.com

Contact Marcia Yudkin: marcia@yudkin.com